Bushcraft Handbook:
Survival techniques

Crafty Ink **Manolo**

INDEX

P 3 **Summary**

P 7 **INTRODUCTION**

P 8 **Chap 1: Introduction to Bushcraft**

P 17 **Chap 2: Construction of a Refuge**

P 27 **Chap 3: Lighting a Fire**

P 35 **Chap 4: Getting Food in Nature**

P 45 **Chap 5: Orientation and Navigation**

P 54 **Chap 6: Water Management**

P 63 **Chap 7: First Aid and Health**

P 72 **Chap 8: Manufacture of Tools and Utensils**

P 80 **Chap 9: Communication and Reporting**

P 89 **Chap 10: Long Term Survival**

P 98 **CONCLUSIONS**

SUMMARY

Chapter 1: Introduction to Bushcraft

- What is bushcraft and why is it important
- History of bushcraft
- Ethics and principles of bushcraft
- Essential bushcraft equipment

Chapter 2: Building a Shelter

- Types of shelters and their uses
- Natural materials for building shelters
- Construction techniques for temporary and permanent shelters
- Shelters for different climatic conditions

Chapter 3: Building a Fire

- Fire lighting techniques
- Selection and preparation of material for the fire
- Fire management and maintenance
- Fire safety and disposal
-

Chapter 4: Getting Food in the Wild

- Identification and collection of edible plants
- Hunting and fishing techniques
- Traps and tools for catching animals
- Storing and cooking food

Chapter 5: Orientation and Navigation

- Use of maps, compass and GPS
- Navigation with the sun, moon and stars
- Orientation techniques using natural signs
- Creating and using routes and landmarks

Chapter 6: Water Management

- Identification and collection of water sources
- Water purification techniques
- Storage and transport of water
- Responsible use of water resources

Chapter 7: First Aid and Health in Bushcraft

- First aid kit for bushcraft
- Treatment of common wounds, bites and stings
- Prevention and treatment of hypothermia and heatstroke
- Management of stress and fatigue in survival situations

Chapter 8: Making Tools and Utensils

- Use and maintenance of knives, axes and saws
- Manufacture of tools and useful objects with natural materials
- Weaving and binding techniques with vegetable fibers
- Construction of containers and vessels

Chapter 9: Communication and Reporting

- Non-verbal communication techniques
- Use of smoke signals, mirrors and other signaling methods
- Creation and interpretation of signs and symbols on the ground
- Use of radios and other communication devices

Chapter 10: Long Term Survival and Life Skills in the Wild

- Planning and organizing a permanent base
- Techniques of agriculture and breeding in the wild nature
- Long-term food storage
- Development of a self-sufficient community in the forest

INTRODUCTION

Bushcraft is an ancient art that involves acquiring and practicing skills and techniques to survive and thrive in nature. This bushcraft handbook has been created to provide a comprehensive and in-depth guide to anyone wishing to learn and develop these essential skills. Through ten detailed chapters, we will explore a wide range of topics, including shelter building, fire-building, finding food and water, orienteering and navigation, first aid, gear and tool making, communication, and long-term survival in the wilderness.

The goal of this manual is to provide a solid foundation of knowledge and practical skills that can be used in a variety of outdoor contexts and situations. Learning to bushcraft can enhance one's experience of nature, foster a sense of self-reliance and resilience, and strengthen the bond between humans and their surroundings.

Chapter 1: Introduction to Bushcraft

1.1 What is bushcraft and why is it important

Bushcraft is the art of living and surviving in nature by exploiting the natural resources that destroy us. The term "bushcraft" derives from the union of the words "bush", which means "bush" or "wild nature", and "craft", which means "art" or "trade". Bushcraft includes a set of skills and techniques that allow a person to live in harmony with the environment, learning to use the available natural resources efficiently and sustainably. This includes building shelters, starting and managing fire, finding and gathering food and water, orienteering and navigation, first aid and health care, making tools and utensils, communication and reporting,

Bushcraft is important for several reasons. First of all, it allows us to develop a deep connection with nature and to understand our place in the natural world. Bushcraft teaches us to respect the environment and to value the resources that the Earth offers us. Furthermore, the skills learned in bushcraft can be useful in emergency or survival situations, allowing us to react effectively to unforeseen challenges. Finally, bushcraft can be a source of personal growth and the development of problem solving skills, resilience and self-discipline.

1.2 History of bushcraft The roots of bushcraft go back to the beginning of human history, when our ancestors lived in close relationship with nature and depended on their survival skills to forage for food, build shelter and defend themselves from danger. Over the millennia, indigenous peoples around the world have developed unique techniques and knowledge to live in harmony with their environments, making the most of the resources at their disposal. These ancient survival traditions have influenced the development of modern bushcraft, which seeks to preserve and disseminate these skills and knowledge.

In the 20th century, bushcraft began to gain popularity as a recreational practice and as a study discipline. Pioneers of modern bushcraft include the likes of Tom Brown Jr., Mors Kochanski and Ray Mears, who have helped spread bushcraft skills and knowledge through books, courses and television programmes. Today, bushcraft is enjoyed by enthusiasts all over the world, both as a hobby and as a way of life, and continues to inspire new generations

of explorers and adventurers.

1.3 Ethics and principles of bushcraft

The bushcraft ethic is based on respect for nature and an awareness of our impact on the environment. Practicing bushcraft means trying to minimize our ecological impact and to use natural resources in a sustainable and responsible way. Some key tenets of bushcraft ethics include:

- Respect for life: All life forms, including plants and animals, deserve respect and consideration. Avoid needlessly damaging the environment and try to act responsibly and consciously.

- Take Only What You Need: When using natural resources for food, water, shelter, or tools, it's important to take only what is absolutely necessary. This approach allows you to conserve resources for the future and minimize the impact on the ecosystem.

- Leave as little impact as possible: The goal of bushcraft is to live in harmony with nature, which means trying to minimize the impact of our actions on the environment. This includes practices such as dispersing fire ashes properly, using trails and campsites responsibly, and complying with local laws and regulations.

- Knowledge sharing: Bushcraft is all about sharing knowledge and skills through teaching and learning. Sharing your knowledge with others is vital to preserving and spreading bushcraft traditions.

- Personal Responsibility: Bushcrafting requires a high degree of personal responsibility. It is important to be well prepared, have the necessary skills and knowledge and be aware of the limits of one's abilities.

1.4 Indispensable essential for bushcraft

However bushcraft focuses on using natural resources, it is important to have basic equipment with you that can facilitate survival and work in the wild. Here is a list of essential bushcraft equipment:

- Knife: A quality knife is an indispensable tool in bushcraft. It can be used for chopping wood, preparing food, building shelters, and working on various projects. Choose a sturdy knife that fits your needs.

- Ax or Saw: An ax or saw can be useful for chopping firewood, felling trees, and building structures. Choose a tool that is suitable for your needs and capabilities.

- Compass and Map: Navigating the bush requires a sense of direction and the ability to use a compass and map. Always have a compass and a map of your area with you, even if you are using a GPS or electronic navigation device.

- Backpack: A sturdy and comfortable backpack is essential for carrying equipment, food and water. Choose a backpack that fits the type of excursion or adventure you intend to undertake.

- Appropriate clothing and footwear: Dressing appropriately is essential to deal with the various climatic and environmental conditions that may be encountered while bushcrafting. Choose clothing and footwear that is resistant, comfortable and suitable for the specific conditions.

- First Aid Kit: A well-stocked first aid kit is essential in dealing with any medical emergencies. Be sure to include items such as bandages, gauze, disinfectant, tweezers, and a thermometer, as well as any personal medications.

- Rope or paracord: Rope is an extremely versatile tool in bushcraft, used for tying, lifting, hauling, and building structures. Paracord is a popular choice due to its strength and light weight.

- Means of Making a Fire: Having several methods at hand for making a fire is critical in bushcraft. Carry waterproof matches, a flint and a windproof lighter.

- Water Container: A durable, reusable water container is essential for transporting and storing drinking water. Choose a container that suits your needs and environmental conditions.

- Thermal blanket or sleeping bag: A light and compact thermal blanket or sleeping bag can be useful to protect yourself from the cold and humidity during the night.

- Food and kitchenware:
  Bring high-energy, long-life
  foods, such as energy bars,
  dried fruit, and freeze-dried
  foods. Also include basic
  cooking utensils, such as a
  pot, portable stove, and
  cutlery.

This list of essential equipment can vary according to personal needs and preferences, as well as specific environmental conditions. It is important to tailor your equipment to your skills and the situations you expect to face while bushcrafting.

With the introduction to complete bushcraft, the subsequent chapters of this manual will explore in detail the skills and techniques necessary to live and survive in the wilderness. Learning and practicing these skills can be a rewarding and fulfilling adventure, providing an opportunity to discover more about ourselves and the world around us.

Chapter 2: Building a Shelter

2.1 Types of shelters and their uses

Building a shelter is one of the fundamental skills of bushcraft, as it offers protection from the elements and a safe place to rest and sleep. There are several types of shelters that can be built from natural materials, each with their own advantages and disadvantages. Listed below are some common types of shelters and their main characteristics:

1. Lean-to (cantilevered shelter): This type of shelter consists of an inclined structure leaning against a support, such as a tree or log. It is relatively easy to build and offers good protection from rain and wind.

2. Tarp: A tarp is a waterproof tarp that can be used to create a quick and versatile shelter. It can be suspended between trees or leaned against natural structures offering protection from the sun, rain and wind.

3. Debris Hut: A debris shelter is a shelter built from branches, leaves, and other natural debris. It offers great thermal insulation and protection from the elements, but can take time and energy to build.

4. Quinzhee or snow igloo: These shelters are built with blocks of compacted snow and are especially suited to winter conditions. They offer excellent thermal insulation, but take time and effort to build.

5. Log Cabin: A log cabin is a more permanent shelter built with woven wooden logs and insulating material covers. It takes time, skill and effort to build, but offers lasting protection from the elements.

2.2 Natural materials for building shelters

Choosing the right materials is essential for building an effective and resistant shelter. Recommended natural materials used in the construction of bushcraft shelters include:

1. Branches and Logs:
Branches and logs can be used as structural supports for most shelters. With sturdy and straight branches to ensure the stability of the shelter.

2. Leaves and debris: Leaves, grass, and other natural debris can be used as insulation and waterproofing material for shelters. They create an insulating layer that protects against cold, humidity and wind.

3. Bark: The bark of some trees can be used as a waterproof covering for shelters. Some types of bark, such as birch and cedar, are particularly strong and flexible, making them suitable for this purpose.

4. Moss: Moss can be used as an insulation and waterproofing material. It has excellent insulating properties and can be easily picked up and applied to shelters.

5. Snow: Snow can be used to build shelters such as quinzhees or igloos, which offer excellent thermal insulation. Compacted snow can be cut into blocks and stacked to create strong walls and ceilings.

2.3 Shelter construction techniques

Shelter construction techniques vary depending on the type of shelter you want to build and the materials available. Some basic techniques that can be used in building different types of shelters are described below:

1. Building a Lean-To: To build a lean-to, start by finding solid support, such as a tree or fallen log. Place a long branch horizontally along the stand and secure it with rope or braid. Then, place the shorter branches at an angle along the horizontal branch, creating a cantilevered structure. Cover the structure with leaves, grass, or bark to create a waterproof, insulating roof.

2. Setting up a tarp: To set up a tarp, you can use ropes to suspend the tarp between two trees or rest it on a natural structure such as a trunk or branch. Be sure to hold the tarp so that rainwater can drain easily and does not pool on the tarp.

3. Building a Debris Hut: Start building an A-shaped structure using branches and logs. Secure a long branch between two supports and place shorter branches alongside the main branch to create an inclined structure. Next, cover the structure with debris such as leaves, grass and moss, creating an insulating layer at least 30-45cm thick. Finally, cover the shelter with branches and logs to keep debris in place and increase structural strength.

4. Building a Quinzhee or Snow Igloo: To build a snow shelter, start by digging an area out of the snow and compacting the snow with your feet or tools. Next, cut blocks of compacted snow and stack them to create walls and a ceiling. Be sure to leave an opening for entry and a small opening for ventilation. Finally, cover the inside walls of the shelter with snow to seal any gaps and increase thermal insulation.

5. Building a Log Cabin: To build a log cabin, start by selecting wood logs of similar length and thickness. Place the logs on top of each other, interlacing them in the corners to create a solid structure. Be sure to leave space for windows and entry. Use insulating material, such as moss or bark, to fill any gaps between logs and improve thermal insulation. Finally, build a sloping roof using branches, logs, and waterproof material like bark or leaves.

2.4 Considerations on the location of the shelter

The location of the shelter is a crucial factor in ensuring its effectiveness and safety. When choosing a location to build a shelter keep, consider the following factors:

1. Protection from the Elements: Choose a location that offers natural protection from wind, rain, and snow. This can include areas sheltered by trees, rocks or other landscape features.

2. Safety: Make sure the location of the shelter is safe and away from potential hazards, such as falling branches, landslides, avalanches or floods.

3. Access to Water: Choose a location near a source of potable water, such as a river, lake, or stream. However, avoid building your shelter too close to water, as this could increase the risk of flooding or moisture.

4. Sun Exposure: If possible, locate the shelter so that it receives sun during the day. This will help keep the shelter warm and dry and will make cooking and drying clothes and equipment easier.

5. Visibility and Signaling: If you are in an emergency situation and need to be located by first responders, place the shelter in a visible area and use signals such as fires, mirrors or bright colors to attract attention.

2.5 Maintenance and repair of shelters

Once the shelter is built, it is important to monitor its condition and make any necessary repairs to ensure its effectiveness and safety. This may include:

1. Frequently check the stability and structural integrity of the shelter, making sure there are no damaged or weakened parts.

2. Replace or repair any insulation or waterproofing materials that have deteriorated or been damaged.

3. Check that the shelter's ventilation system is functioning and that there is no accumulation of condensation or humidity inside the shelter.

4. Remove any debris or fallen branches that may obstruct entry or compromise the safety of the shelter.

5. Check that the area around the shelter is free of hazards, such as ice formations, snow accumulations or overhanging branches.

6. maintain a fire close to the shelter to warm it and mark the location, but ensure it is far enough away and protected to avoid accidental fires.

In summary, Chapter 2 of this bushcraft manual focused on building shelters, a critical skill for surviving and thriving in the wilderness. Different types of shelters, natural materials used in shelter construction, basic construction techniques, shelter location considerations, and shelter maintenance and repair tips were discussed. Mastering these skills is essential for anyone who practices bushcraft, as proper shelter can mean the difference between life and death in survival situations.

In later chapters of this manual, we will explore other fundamental bushcraft skills and techniques, including building a fire, finding and purifying water, hunting and fishing, cooking and preserving food, navigating and first aid techniques.

Chapter 3: Building a Fire

3.1 Introduction to starting a fire

Fire-making is one of the most important skills in bushcraft, as fire provides warmth, light, protection, the ability to cook food and purify water. In this chapter we will explore different fire starting techniques, fire material selection and preparation, fire management and maintenance, and fire safety and disposal tips.

3.2 Fire lighting techniques

There are several techniques for starting a fire, each with its own advantages and disadvantages. Some of the most common techniques are described below:

1. Lighter or matches: Lighters and matches are the simplest and most efficient tools for starting a fire. However, they can be affected by humidity and require a supply of fuel or spare matches.

2. Magnifying Glass: Using a magnifying glass or other clear, convex object, sunlight can be focused on a specific point, generating enough heat to ignite the combustible material. This method requires a direct sunlight source and can take time and experience to master.

3. Steel and flint: Steel and flint are a classic tool for starting a fire. Striking the flint against the flint produces sparks which can be directed at a combustible material to start a fire. This method is reliable and works even in wet conditions, but requires practice and experience to master.

4. Bow and Drill: The bow and drill is a traditional fire-starting technique that uses friction to generate heat. The drill is a sharp stick that is rotated rapidly in the hands or with the help of a bow, while being pressed against a wooden base. This method takes time, effort and practice to master, but can be very effective once you learn it.

5. Battery and Steel Wool: By connecting the terminals of a battery to steel wool, an electric current is generated which causes the wool to heat up and ignite. This technique is quick and easy, but requires a working battery and steel wool.

3.3 Selection and preparation of material for fire

Choosing and preparing the right fire material is essential to ensure rapid ignition and a stable fire. Fire materials can be divided into three main categories: kindling, small wood, and large wood.

1. Igniter: The igniter is a lightweight, highly flammable material that is easily ignited with a spark or flame. Natural igniters can include birch bark, plant fluff, dry leaves, dry grass, dry mosses and lichens. Artificial igniters, such as cotton dipped in petroleum jelly or steel wool, can be useful in emergency situations or when natural igniters are hard to find.

2. Small Wood: Small wood consists of thin branches and dry twigs that will burn rapidly once the kindler is lit. This wood is essential in helping to establish the fire and preparing it to burn the larger wood. It's important to pick up a variety of sizes, from as thin as a hair to as thick as a finger.

3. Large Wood: Large wood consists of thicker branches and logs that will burn longer and provide a constant, hot fire. This wood should be harvested dry and, if possible, split to expose the dry wood inside. It's important to pick up a variety of sizes, from as thick as a wrist to larger logs.

Once you've gathered your materials for the fire, it's important to properly prepare the fire area. Choose an area that is flat and free of flammable debris, such as dry grass or leaves. Create a platform of stones or packed earth to isolate the fire from the ground and reduce the risk of accidental fires. Also, make sure you have a source of water or earth on hand to put out the fire in case of an emergency.

3.4 Fire management and maintenance

Once a fire is lit, it is important to manage and maintain it properly to ensure it provides heat and light efficiently and safely. Some fire management and maintenance tips include:

1. Feed the fire small and large wood gradually, adding more wood only when necessary to maintain the desired size and intensity of the fire.

2. Keep the fire well ventilated, making sure air can circulate freely around the base of the fire and between the pieces of wood.

3. Use tools such as sticks or stones to move and rearrange the wood in the fire, helping to ensure an even burn and reducing smoke build-up.

4. Monitor the fire closely, making sure it doesn't accidentally spread to surrounding areas or become too large and uncontrollable.

3.5 Safety and fire disposal

Safety is of paramount importance when it comes to fire in bushcraft. Follow these guidelines to ensure safety and prevent accidents or damage to the environment:

1. Never leave a fire unattended. Ensure that someone is always present to monitor the fire and intervene if there is a problem.

2. keep a safe distance between the fire and flammable objects, such as tents, sleeping bags or equipment.

3. Forbidden to light fires in strong wind conditions or in areas with high fire risk, such as dry grasslands or forests during the fire season.

4. Do not start a fire near trees with low branches or in an area with an abundance of flammable debris on the ground.

5. Always have a source of water or earth on hand to put out the fire in an emergency.

When it's time to dispose of the fire, follow these steps to do it in a safe and environmentally friendly way:

1. Let the fire burn naturally until only ash and embers remain.

2. Slowly pour water over the embers, making sure to thoroughly moisten the fire area. Stir the ashes and arms with a stick to ensure they are thoroughly wet and there are no hidden hot spots.

3. Wait for the fire area to cool completely to the touch. This may take some time, especially if the fire has been burning for several hours.

4. Once the fire area is cool, remove the ashes and scatter them over a larger area, away from waterways or sensitive areas. If possible, return the fire area to its natural state by covering it with earth or stones.

In summary, Chapter 3 of this bushcraft manual has listed the importance of fire starting and provided an overview of fire starting techniques, fire material selection and preparation, fire management and maintenance, and fire safety and disposal. Mastery of these skills is essential for anyone who practices bushcraft, as fire is an essential resource for survival and well-being in the wilderness.

In subsequent chapters of this manual, we will continue to explore other key bushcraft skills, including finding and purifying water, hunting and fishing, cooking and preserving food, navigation and first aid techniques.

Chapter 4: Getting Food in the Wild

4.1 Introduction to gathering food in nature

In bushcraft, knowing how to forage for food in the wild is a critical skill for long-term survival. In this chapter, we will explore the different sources of food that can be found in nature, such as identifying and harvesting edible plants, hunting and fishing techniques, using traps and tools to capture animals, and methods for storing and cooking food.

4.2 Identification and collection of edible plants

Edible plants are a vital food source in the wild, providing nutrients, energy and fiber. However, it is essential to know which plants are edible and which are poisonous or toxic. Here are some tips for identifying and harvesting edible plants:

1. Study local edible plant guides and manuals before setting out on a bushcraft adventure. Familiarize yourself with the plants in the area and their characteristics, such as the shape of the leaves, the color of the flowers and the appearance of the fruit.

2. Learn to distinguish edible plants from similar poisonous plants. Some poisonous plants can look a lot like edible ones, so it's important to know the key differences to avoid accidental poisoning.

3. Only harvest plants that you are 100% sure of edibility. If you're not entirely sure of a plant's identity, it's best to leave it alone.

4. Watch for signs of contamination, such as pollution, pesticides, or bacteria. Don't pick plants near busy roads, polluted waterways, or in agricultural areas that may use pesticides.

5. Collect responsibly, taking
only what is necessary and
trying not to damage the local
ecosystem. Forbidden to
collect rare or endangered
plants and to take only a small
part of each plant to allow it to
continue growing.

Some examples of common edible
plants include dandelions, nettles,
lampascione, blueberries and porcini
mushrooms. However, edible plants
vary greatly by region and season, so
it's important to research local
species and the best times to harvest
them.

4.3 Hunting and fishing techniques

Hunting and fishing are other
important food sources in the
wilderness, providing protein, fat, and
other essential nutrients. There are
several hunting and fishing
techniques that can be used in
bushcraft, including:

1. Bow and Arrow Hunting: The bow and arrows are traditional hunting tools that can be crafted using natural materials found in the wilderness. Bow hunting requires practice and skill, but it is an effective and silent method of hunting animals of various sizes.

2. Slingshot: The slingshot is another simple hunting tool that can be easily constructed using rubber bands, leather, or synthetic materials. Slingshots can be used to hunt small animals, such as birds and squirrels, by throwing small stones or projectiles with precision.

3. Hand Fishing: Hand fishing is catching fish directly with your hands, usually in shallow water or near rocks and other hiding places. This technique takes patience and skill, but can be an effective way to get food if you don't have fishing gear.

4. Angling: Angling is one of the most common fishing techniques and can be done with a variety of gear, including makeshift fishing rods, homemade hooks, and natural bait. Angling requires patience and knowledge of fish behavior, such as their feeding times and their preferences for bait.

5. Spearing: Spearing is a hunting and fishing technique that consists of ringing and catching animals with a spear or harpoon. This method can be used to hunt land animals, such as deer or wild boar, or to fish for large fish, such as salmon or barracuda.

4.4 Traps and tools for trapping animals

Traps and gear are useful tools for catching animals in bushcraft, allowing you to capture prey without having to be constantly present. There are many types of traps and gear, including:

1. Snap Traps: Snap traps are mechanical devices that activate when an animal disturbs a trigger or lever, quickly catching it. Examples of snap traps include furry animal traps and bird traps.

2. Leg Traps: Leg traps consist of a loop of rope or wire that tightens around the animal as it enters the trap. These traps can be used to catch small animals, such as rabbits or squirrels.

3. Fish Nets and Traps: Fish nets and traps are devices that trap fish when they swim inside. Examples of these devices include fishing nets, pots and shrimp traps. These tools can be constructed from natural or synthetic materials and placed in high fish traffic areas to increase the chances of success.

4. Pits and Pitfall Traps: Pits and Pitfall Traps are devices that use gravity to trap animals. These traps may include holes dug in the ground with sharp spikes in the bottom, weighted pit traps, or platform traps that collapse under the weight of the animal. These traps can be effective for catching animals of various sizes, but require strategic location and good cover to be effective.

4.5 Storing and cooking food

Once food has been procured in the wild, it is important to know how to store and cook it properly to ensure its safety and nutritional value. Below are some methods of preserving and cooking food in bushcraft:

1. Drying: Drying is a method of preserving food that involves removing water from food products, reducing the growth of bacteria and molds. Meat, fish, fruit and vegetables can be dried in the sun, over the smoke of a fire or in an improvised dryer built with branches and leaves.

2. Smoking: Smoking is a method of preserving and cooking food that uses wood smoke to add flavor and extend the shelf life of foods. Meat and fish can be smoked over an open fire or in a makeshift smokehouse built from branches and leaves.

3. Hot Stone Cooking: Hot stone cooking is a traditional cooking method that uses fire-heated stones to cook foods. This method can be used to cook meat, fish, vegetables, and bread, and requires only flat, heat-resistant stones.

4. Boiling and stewing: Boiling and stewing are cooking methods that use water or other liquids to cook food slowly and evenly. These methods can be used to make soups, stews, and risottos, and require only a heatproof pot or container.

5. Grilling and Roasting:
Grilling and roasting are high-temperature cooking methods that use the direct heat of a fire to cook food. These methods are ideal for cooking meat, fish and vegetables, and can be achieved using improvised grills, skewers or simply placing the food directly on the embers.

In conclusion, Chapter 4 of this bushcraft manual has explored how to forage food in the wild, covering the identification and gathering of edible plants, hunting and fishing techniques, using traps and tools to catch animals, and the methods of storing and cooking food. Knowing and mastering these skills is critical to surviving and thriving in a natural environment, particularly during long-term bushcraft adventures.

It's important to remember that practice makes perfect, and learning these skills takes time, patience, and dedication. Furthermore, it is essential to respect the natural environment and local ecosystems, by gathering and hunting responsibly and sustainably. Finally, never forget the importance of personal safety and hygiene precautions when gathering, preparing and cooking food in the wilderness.

With these acquired skills and the awareness of the resulting responsibilities, one is ready to face the challenges of bushcraft and to experience the satisfaction of living in harmony with nature, providing nourishment and sustenance through the resources that the earth offers. Keep refining your skills and exploring new techniques so you can become increasingly self-reliant and in tune with your surroundings.

Chapter 5: Orientation and Navigation

5.1 Introduction to orientation and navigation

Navigation and navigation are essential skills for any bushcraft adventure, enabling you to navigate the wilderness safely and find your way back home. In this chapter, we will explore several methods of orientation and navigation, including using maps, compasses, and GPS, navigating by the sun, moon, and stars, using natural signs, and creating and using routes and landmarks.

5.2 Use of maps, compass and GPS

Maps, compasses, and GPS are common navigation tools that can be used to determine location, direction, and distance between two points. Below are some tips for using these tools in bushcraft:

1. Maps: Topographic maps are detailed maps that show physical terrain features, such as hills, valleys, rivers, and trails. Knowing how to read a topographic map is critical to bushcraft navigation. Familiarize yourself with map legends, contour lines, and other symbols used to represent terrain features.

2. Compass: A compass is a navigational instrument that indicates the direction of magnetic north. Using a compass in conjunction with a topographical map allows you to determine the direction and distance between two points and to follow a predetermined route. Learn how to use a compass, including adjusting magnetic declination and triangulating your location.

3. GPS: GPS (Global Positioning System) is a satellite navigation system that provides location and time information around the world. GPS devices can be used in bushcraft to determine your exact location, follow routes, and record points of interest. However, it is important not to rely solely on GPS devices, as they can fail, drain battery or lose satellite signal.

5.3 Navigate by sun, moon and stars

Celestial navigation is the art of using the sun, moon, and stars to determine position and direction. These techniques can be used as backup navigation methods when modern tools are unavailable or fail to work. Here are some celestial navigation techniques useful in bushcraft:

1. Sun: The sun rises in the east and sets in the west, with its highest point in the sky at noon. Use the sun's shadow to determine east-west direction by placing a vertical stick in the ground and watching the shadow cast. The direction of the shadow is approximately east-west. You can also use an analog watch to determine south: point the hour hand at the sun and imagine an imaginary line midway between the hour hand and the number 12. This line will point south in the northern hemisphere and north in the southern hemisphere.

2. Moon: The moon can be used to determine east-west direction based on its phase and position in the sky. During a waxing moon, the illuminated edge of the moon forms an arch pointing east, while during a waning moon, the arch points west. When the moon is high in the sky, its position can be used to estimate the north-south direction.

3. Stars: Stars can be used to determine north and south by locating specific constellations and stars that indicate the celestial pole. In the Northern Hemisphere, look for the North Star (Polaris), which is near the Earth's axis of rotation and points north. In the Southern Hemisphere, look for the Southern Cross and the two stars called The Pointers, which indicate roughly celestial south.

5.4 Orientation techniques using natural signs

In addition to navigation tools and celestial techniques, natural markings can be used to help determine direction and maintain bearings in bushcraft. Here are some examples of natural signs useful for navigation:

1. Plant Growth: Plants tend to grow in the direction of sunlight, which can provide clues about the east-west direction. For example, mosses tend to grow on the moist, shady side of trees and rocks, which in the northern hemisphere is usually the north side.

2. Terrain Formations: Terrain features, such as hills, rivers, and ridges, can be used as reference points for navigation and to determine direction. For example, rivers tend to flow downstream and generally out to sea, which can help establish the general direction of movement.

3. Wind: Wind can provide clues about direction, particularly in areas where the prevailing winds blow consistently from a specific direction. Observing the direction of the wind and its interactions with plants and soil can help determine its direction.

5.5 Creating and using routes and landmarks

In bushcraft, it is important to create and use routes and landmarks to aid navigation and prevent loss. Here are some tips for creating and using routes and landmarks:

1. Routes: Choosing routes that follow natural terrain features, such as rivers, ridgelines or animal trails, can make navigation easier and reduce the risk of getting lost. However, it is important to be aware of the potential dangers and difficulties associated with these routes, such as rough terrain, wildlife or adverse weather conditions.

2. Landmarks: Landmarks are easily recognizable terrain features, such as mountains, lakes, trees, or rocks, that you can use to orient yourself and follow a route. When choosing a landmark, make sure it is visible from different angles and distances, and that it is distinct from other surrounding features.

3. Marking: Natural or artificial signs and symbols can be used to mark a route and facilitate navigation. For example, you can create a path of stones or branches, make incisions in trees or rocks, or build temporary structures such as cairns or cairns. However, it is important to respect the natural surroundings and remove any man-made markings once your bushcraft adventure is over.

4. Annotating and Sketching: Taking notes and sketching terrain features and landmarks can help you remember navigational information and plan future routes. Use a waterproof notebook or smartphone application to record this information.

In conclusion, Chapter 5 of this Bushcraft Handbook explored various orienteering and navigation techniques, including the use of maps, compasses and GPS, navigating by sun, moon and stars, using natural signs and the creation and use of routes and landmarks. Developing and honing these skills is essential to ensure safe and successful bushcraft and outdoor adventure sailing.

It is important to practice these techniques regularly and under different conditions to build confidence in your sailing skills. In addition, it is essential to be prepared for the unexpected and to always have a backup plan available, such as carrying a map and compass even when using a GPS. Finally, remember to respect the natural environment and practice the "leave no trace" ethic when bushcrafting.

Chapter 6: Water Management

6.1 Introduction to water management

Water is a vital resource for human survival, and water management is a crucial component of bushcraft. In this chapter, we will explore how to identify and harvest water sources, purify water for drinking, conserve and transport water, and use water resources responsibly.

6.2 Identifying and harvesting water sources

Natural water sources can be found in a variety of environments, and knowing them is essential to ensuring a constant supply of water on bushcraft adventures. Here are some common water sources and tips for collecting them:

1. Rivers, Streams and Streams: Flowing water is often the most accessible and reliable source of water. However, make sure the water comes from a clean source and is not contaminated with chemicals or bacteria. It is forbidden to draw water near human settlements, industrial plants or agricultural areas.

2. Lakes and Ponds: While lakes and ponds can provide large amounts of water, the water is likely to be stagnant and potentially contaminated. When drawing water from these sources, try to draw it from the surface, away from the shore, and purify it before drinking.

3. Springs: Natural springs are sources of clean water that bubble up from the ground. The water from the springs is often cold, clear and drinkable without treatment, but it is still advisable to purify it as a precaution.

4. Rain: Rainwater harvesting is a simple and effective method of obtaining potable water. Use tarps, ponchos, or other impermeable receptacles to catch any falling water, and make sure the collection system is clean and free of contaminants.

5. Dew and Moisture: Water from dew or moisture can be collected using sponges, cloths, or other absorbent materials. Wrap the material around plants or grass and squeeze it into a container to catch the water.

6. Snow and Ice: Snow and ice can be melted to make potable water, but it's important to do it slowly and carefully to avoid cold burns or hypothermia. Also, make sure the snow or ice is clean and not contaminated with chemicals or bacteria.

6.3 Water purification techniques

Water purification is a vital step in ensuring the safety and potability of collected water. Several purification techniques can be used to remove impurities, bacteria and viruses from water:

1. Boiling: Boiling water is one of the simplest and most effective methods of purifying water. Bring the water to a boil and boil it for at least one minute to kill most bacteria and parasites. However, boiling will not remove any heavy chemicals or pollutants.

2. Filtration: There are various water filtration devices available, ranging from activated carbon filters to ultrafine porosity membrane filters. These filters can remove particles, bacteria, protozoa and, in some cases, viruses from the water. It is important to follow the manufacturer's instructions for the use and proper maintenance of the filter.

3. Chemical disinfection: The use of chemicals, such as chlorine or iodine, can be an effective method of purifying water. Follow the manufacturer's instructions for proper mixing and contact time to ensure proper purification. However, some chemicals can leave an unpleasant taste in the water and are not effective against some resistant parasites, such as Cryptosporidium.

4. UV Disinfection: Disinfection with ultraviolet (UV) light is an effective method of killing bacteria, viruses and protozoa. There are portable UV disinfection devices that can be used to treat water while bushcrafting. However, UV disinfection may be less effective in cloudy water or water with a high concentration of particles.

6.4 Storage and transport of water

Storing and transporting water safely and efficiently is vital to ensuring a constant supply of water during your bushcraft adventures. Here are some tips for storing and transporting water:

1. Containers: Use water containers that are resistant, impermeable and easy to clean. The flexible, collapsible containers are ideal for bushcraft, as they can be folded up and stored easily when not in use.

2. Sunlight Protection: Store water out of direct sunlight to reduce algae and bacteria growth. Use opaque containers or cover clear containers with a tarp or cloth.

3. Cleaning and Disinfection: Clean water containers regularly with soap and water, and disinfect them with a diluted bleach solution or water purification tablets to prevent contamination and bacterial growth.

4. Transport: When transporting water, make sure that the containers are tightly closed and placed in a stable position inside the backpack or cargo. Use straps or ropes to secure containers and reduce the risk of leakage or breakage.

5. Rationing: In situations where the water supply is limited, it may be necessary to ration the water to ensure it lasts as long as necessary. Establish a daily water consumption plan and stick to it as much as possible. Remember to consider physical activities and weather conditions, which can affect water needs.

6.5 Responsible use of water resources

The practice of bushcraft involves respecting and conserving the natural environment, and this includes the responsible use of water resources. Here are some tips for using water responsibly:

1. Drink water sparingly: Use only the amount of water needed for drinking, cooking and personal hygiene. Reduce water waste by reusing cooking water for washing dishes or collecting rainwater for non-potable purposes.

2. Protect water sources: Avoid contaminating water sources with chemicals, human waste, or other pollutants. Use biodegradable products for washing dishes and the body, and practice human waste disposal techniques at an appropriate distance from water sources.

3. Respect Aquatic Life: Do not disturb aquatic ecosystems and wildlife that depend on water sources. Do not fish or swim in protected waters or animal breeding areas.

4. Sharing resources: In situations where water resources are limited, it is important to cooperate and share water with other bushcrafters or hikers. Communicate and collaborate with others to ensure that everyone has access to an adequate supply of water.

In conclusion, Chapter 6 of this bushcraft handbook explored water stewardship, including techniques for identifying and harvesting water sources, purifying water, conserving and transporting water, and using water resources responsibly . Effective water management is critical to survival and success in bushcraft and outdoor adventures.

Chapter 7: First Aid and Health in Bushcraft

7.1 Introduction to bushcraft first aid and health

Health and first aid are vital aspects of bushcrafting, as the ability to deal with and manage medical emergencies and common health problems can mean the difference between a manageable situation and a potentially dangerous one. In this chapter, we will explore the essential components of a bushcraft first aid kit, treating common wounds, bites and stings, preventing and treating hypothermia and heatstroke, and managing stress and fatigue in survival situations.

7.2 First aid kit for bushcraft

A well-stocked first aid kit is an essential to any bushcraft adventure. The following items are recommended for a basic first aid kit:

1. Adhesive bandages of various sizes and shapes, to cover cuts and abrasions.
2. Sterile gauze to cover larger wounds or to plug bleeding.
3. Medical adhesive tape for fixing gauzes and bandages.

4. Tweezers for removing thorns, splinters or ticks.
5. Scissors for cutting folds, gauze or clothing.
6. Disposable nitrile gloves to protect hands when dispensing first aid.
7. Antiseptic solution, such as povidone iodine or chlorhexidine, to disinfect wounds.
8. Antibiotic cream to prevent infection in wounds.
9. Butterfly patches for closing deep cuts.
10.	Elastic bandages to support sprains or dislocations.
11.	Triangular bandage to immobilize fractures or create an improvised handkerchief.
12.	Emergency blanket to keep warm or protect from the sun.
13.	Painkillers, such as acetaminophen or ibuprofen, to relieve pain and reduce inflammation.
14.	Antihistamines for the treatment of allergic reactions.

15.	Hemostatic forceps to control bleeding in case of serious injuries.

16.	Irrigation syringe for cleaning wounds.

17.	A first aid manual for references and instructions.

7.3 Treatment of common wounds, bites and stings

While bushcrafting, a number of common wounds and bites can be encountered. Here are some general guidelines for treating these situations:

1. Cuts and abrasions: Clean the wound with clean water and soap or an antiseptic solution. Apply an antibiotic cream and cover with a tight bandage or gauze.

2. Animal bites: Wash the wound with soap and water, apply an antiseptic and cover with gauze. Seek medical help if the bite is from a wild animal, as you may need tetanus or rabies prophylaxis.

3. Snakebites: Warm calm and limit movement of the affected limb to reduce the spread of venom. Remove any jewelry or tight clothing, but avoid cutting the wound or aspirating the venom. Do not apply ice or a tourniquet. Seek medical assistance immediately.

4. Insect bites: Apply a topical antihistamine or hydrocortisone cream to relieve itching and swelling. If you experience a serious allergic reaction, such as difficulty breathing or swelling of your face, seek medical help right away.

5. Ticks: Use tweezers to grasp the tick as close to the skin as possible and gently pull straight up, avoiding squeezing or twisting the body of the tick. After removing the tick, disinfect the area with an antiseptic and wash your hands with soap and water. Monitor the bite site for signs of infection and see a doctor if symptoms such as fever, rash, or joint pain develop.

7.4 Prevention and treatment of hypothermia and heatstroke

Hypothermia and heatstroke are due to potentially dangerous conditions that can occur while bushcrafting. It's important to know the symptoms and treatments for these conditions, as well as how to prevent them.

1. Hypothermia: Hypothermia occurs when the body temperature drops below normal due to exposure to cold. Symptoms include chills, confusion, slurred speech, lethargy, and in severe cases, loss of consciousness. To prevent hypothermia, wear weather-appropriate clothing, keep your body dry, and consume warm food and drink. To treat hypothermia, move the person to a sheltered location, remove wet clothes, and wrap them in warm blankets or a sleeping bag. Provide hot, sugary drinks, but avoid alcohol and caffeine.

2. Heatstroke: Heatstroke occurs when your body temperature rises rapidly due to exposure to excessive heat. Symptoms include hot, flushed skin, excessive or stopped sweating, nausea, dizziness, and, in severe cases, seizures or loss of consciousness. To prevent heat stroke, wear light, breathable clothing, drink plenty of water and rest in the shade during the hottest hours of the day. To treat heatstroke, move the person to a cool, shaded place, remove excess clothing, and cool the body with cool water or cold packs applied to the armpits, groin, and neck. Provide cool water or sports drinks to rehydrate, but avoid alcohol and caffeine. Seek medical help right away if you have heatstroke, as it can be a life-threatening condition.

7.5 Management of stress and fatigue in survival situations

Bushcraft survival situations can be present and emotionally stressful. It is important to know strategies for managing stress and fatigue in order to maintain mental clarity and preserve physical resources.

1. Planning and Organizing: Having a plan and organizing your daily activities can help reduce stress and ensure you have enough time for rest and recovery.

2. Time Management: Learning to manage time effectively can help reduce stress and ensure that crucial tasks are completed in a timely manner. Prioritize and focus on the most important tasks.

3. Rest and Sleep: Make sure you set aside time for rest and sleep each day. Adequate rest helps maintain mental clarity and allows the body to recover from physical activity.

4. Relaxation Techniques: Practicing relaxation techniques such as deep breathing, meditation, or stretching can help reduce stress and improve mental and emotional well-being.

5. Communication and support: In group situations, communicating openly with other group members and offering mutual support can help reduce stress and strengthen group cohesion.

6. Self-care: Maintaining good personal hygiene, eating adequate nutrition, and meeting your emotional needs can help reduce stress and support resilience in survival situations.

In conclusion, Chapter 7 of this bushcraft manual explored bushcraft first aid and health, including the essential components of a first aid kit, treating common wounds, bites and stings, and preventing and treating hypothermia and heatstroke, and managing stress and fatigue in survival situations. Knowledge and application of these skills can greatly increase the chances of success and safety in bushcraft adventures.

Chapter 8: Making Tools and Utensils

8.1 Introduction to the making of bushcraft tools and utensils

Tool and tool making is a fundamental skill in bushcraft. Being able to craft useful items out of natural materials can be the difference between surviving and thriving in a wild environment. In this chapter we will explore the use and maintenance of knives, axes and saws, how to make tools and useful objects with natural materials, techniques of weaving and binding with vegetable fibers and the construction of containers and vessels.

8.2 Use and maintenance of knives, axes and saws

Knives, axes and saws are essential bushcraft tools. Each tool has its own specific functions and requires proper maintenance to ensure safe and efficient use.

1. Knives: A good quality bushcraft knife is a versatile and indispensable tool. It can be used for a variety of tasks, such as carving, slicing, digging and preparing food. To keep your knife in top condition, it's important to keep it clean and sharp. Clean the knife after each use and oil periodically to prevent rust. Use a whetstone to keep the edge sharp and efficient.

2. Axes: An ax is a useful tool for felling trees and working wood. It is important to choose an ax of the right size and weight for the specific task and your physical strength. To keep your ax in good condition, clean and oil your ax head regularly. Sharpen the ax with a whetstone or specific ax sharpener, maintaining an appropriate sharpening angle.

3. Saws: A saw is an ideal tool for cutting through larger branches and logs. Folding handsaws or portable chainsaws are common options for bushcraft. back up the saw clean and oiled to prevent rust and ensure smooth operation. Replace or sharpen blades when they become dull to ensure precise and efficient cuts.

8.3 Manufacture of tools and useful objects from natural materials

In bushcraft, a variety of useful tools and items can be created using natural materials. Here are some examples:

1. Walking sticks: A sturdy stick can be used as a support when walking, as a pole for setting up a tent or as a defensive weapon against wild animals. Put up a straight, strong branch, remove any secondary branches and strip the bark if necessary. You can carve a comfort handle or wrap it with rope or leather for a better grip.

2. Slingshot: A slingshot is a simple but effective weapon for hunting small animals or for self-defense. To make a slingshot, find a sturdy forked branch and cut a strip of rubber band or leather to connect the two fork ends. You can use a piece of leather or fabric to create a central pocket to insert the piece into.

3. Spear: A spear can be used for hunting, fishing, or defense. Join a straight, sturdy stick and carve a sharp pointed end. To increase the power and effectiveness of the spear, it is possible to add a stone or metal point, fixing it to the stick with rope or vegetable fibres.

4. Hammocks: Hammocks are a great option for sleeping comfortably and safely off the ground. To build a hammock, you can use a fishing net, piece of burlap, or similar material. Tie the ends of the material to two sturdy, appropriately spaced trees, making sure the hammock hangs at least 18 inches off the ground.

8.4 Weaving and binding techniques with vegetable fibers

Plant fibers can be used to make ropes, baskets, rugs, and other useful items. Here are some common braiding and tying techniques:

1. Rope: To create strong rope, gather long, strong plant fibers, such as tree bark, palm leaves, or nettle fiber. Divide the fibers into strands and twist them together, wrapping the strands around each other to create an even, strong cord.

2. Braid Weaving: To make a braid, divide the plant fibers into three strands and braid them, together by passing each strand over the adjacent one in one continuous motion. This technique can be used to create belts, purse handles and other similar items.

3. Basket Weave: Basket weave is a weaving technique used to create baskets, rugs, and other flat objects. Arrange the plant fibers vertically and horizontally, intertwining the fibers so that they cross at right angles. Keep adding fiber until you reach your desired size.

4. Figure-of-eight knot: The figure-of-eight knot is a sturdy and versatile knot that can be used to tie objects together or secure a rope to a fixed point. To tie a figure of eight, loop one end of the rope around the rope, creating a loop. Then, pass the end of the rope back through the loop and tighten the knot.

8.5 Construction of containers and vessels

Crafting containers and vessels using natural materials is a useful skill in bushcraft for storing food, water, and other important items. Here are some ideas for building containers and containers with natural materials:

1. Wooden Bowls: A wooden bowl can be created by carving a piece of wood with a knife or axe. Choose a suitable piece of wood, preferably hardwood, and carve the center of the piece into a bowl of the desired depth and size.

2. Woven Baskets: Woven baskets can be made using plant fibers such as rush, willow, or reed. Cut the fibers into long, thin strips, then weave them together using plaiting techniques such as basket weave or braid braiding. You can create baskets of different shapes and sizes to meet your needs.

3. Bark Containers: The bark of some trees, such as birch or cedar, can be used to make lightweight, water-resistant containers. Carefully peel off a piece of bark from the tree, then fold it over and secure it with rope or plant fibers to create a container. It is important not to excessively damage the trees when harvesting the bark.

4. Empty Gourds or
Watermelons: Empty gourds or
watermelons can be used as
containers for water, food, or
small items. Cut off the top end
of the pumpkin or coconut and
remove the pulp and seeds.
Let the inner shell dry before
container.

In conclusion, Chapter 8 of this
bushcraft handbook explored tool and
tool making, including the use and
maintenance of knives, axes, and
saws, the making of tools and utility
items from natural materials, braiding
techniques, and binding with
vegetable fibers, and the construction
of containers and vessels. Having the
ability to make and maintain the tools
needed for the outdoors is an
essential bushcraft skill, which can
increase your likelihood of survival
and comfort during wilderness
adventures.

Chapter 9: Communication and Reporting

9.1 Introduction to communication and signaling in bushcraft

Communication and signaling are essential bushcraft skills, particularly during emergency situations or when working in a team. Being able to send and receive information effectively can increase the safety and efficiency of outdoor activities. In this chapter we will explore nonverbal communication techniques, the use of smoke signals, mirrors and other signaling methods, the creation and interpretation of signs and symbols on the ground, and the use of radios and other communication devices.

9.2 Non-verbal communication techniques

Nonverbal communication is an effective method of sharing information without making noise or attracting unwanted attention. Some common non-verbal communication techniques in bushcraft include:

1. Gestures: Hands can be used to indicate directions, signal dangers, or send specific messages. For example, a fist may indicate "stop," while a clenched index and middle finger extended may indicate "forward" or "in that direction."

2. Facial Expressions: Facial expressions can convey emotions or responses to specific situations. For example, raising the eyebrows can indicate surprise or interest, while frowning can signal confusion or concern.

3. Body Language: Body language can provide insight into a person's emotional or physical state. For example, an upright, open posture may indicate confidence and readiness for action, while a closed, hunched posture may suggest fear or submission.

4. Nodding: A nod can indicate understanding, agreement, or acknowledgment. For example, a vertical nod can mean "yes" or "understood", while a horizontal nod can mean "no" or "I don't understand".

9.3 Use of smoke signals, mirrors and other signaling methods

In emergency situations or when remote attention needs to be drawn, the use of smoke signals, mirrors and other signaling methods can be vital. Here are some common methods:

1. Smoke Signals: Smoke signals can be used to send long distance messages or to signal your location. To create a smoke signal, build a fire and add moist or green material to produce thick, white smoke. Cover and uncover the fire with a blanket or tarp to create intermittent smoke signals.

2. Mirrors: Mirrors or any reflective surface can be used to send light signals a long distance. To use a mirror to signal, reflect sunlight in the desired direction, moving the mirror to create short flashes. This method can be used to get the attention of rescuers, other groups or individuals.

3. Whistles: A whistle can be used to send sound signals over a distance. Use repeated short puffs to signal your location or request assistance. The sound of the whistle can travel farther than that of the human voice and save energy.

4. Flags and visual cues: Flags, colored cloths, or other visible objects can be used to signal your location or send messages. Place the flag or tarp in an open, conspicuous area, preferably high up, such as in a tree or hill.

9.4 Creation and interpretation of signs and symbols on the ground

Creating and interpreting signs and symbols on the ground can be useful for signaling routes, locations and other important information. Here are some tips for using signs and symbols in bushcraft:

1. Paths: Create paths with stones, branches or other natural objects to mark the path to a destination or to mark the passage of the group. Make sure the signs are clear and easily recognizable.

2. Terrain Symbols: Use natural objects to create symbols on the ground that convey specific messages, such as directions, warnings, or calls for help. For example, an arrow made of stones can indicate a direction, while a circle with a cross in the center can signal danger or an area to avoid.

3. Marking on Trees or Rocks:
Use a knife, piece of coal, or
rock to mark symbols on trees
or rocks. These signs can be
used to indicate routes, identify
places of interest or signal
messages to those who find
them.

9.5 Use of Radios and Other
Communication Devices

In some situations, the use of radios
and other communication devices can
be essential to maintain contact with
the group or call for help in an
emergency. Here are some common
communication devices in bushcraft:

1. Portable Radios: Portable
radios, such as walkie-talkies,
are an effective way to
maintain group contact or
communicate with other people
at a distance. Having a set of
radios with good range and
spare batteries is crucial.

2. Satellite Phones: Satellite phones are communication devices that use satellites to establish a telephone connection in remote areas or areas without cell coverage. They can be used to call for help in an emergency or to communicate with people outside the bushcraft area. However, it's important to remember that satellite phones can be expensive and require a subscription to operate.

3. GPS Messaging Devices: GPS messaging devices, such as the Garmin inReach, allow you to send and receive text messages via satellite. These devices can also provide GPS location information and allow you to share your location with friends, family, or emergency responders. They require a subscription and can be useful in emergencies or for communicating with people outside the bushcraft area.

4. Shortwave Radio: Shortwave radios are communication devices that use long-range radio frequencies to transmit and receive messages. These radios can be used to communicate long distance, listen to news and weather information, and contact emergency responders. However, shortwave radios can be complex to use and require some knowledge of frequencies and transmission techniques.

In conclusion, Chapter 9 of this bushcraft handbook has explored the importance of communication and signaling in bushcraft, including non-verbal communication techniques, the use of smoke signals, mirrors and other signaling methods, the creation and the interpretation of signs and symbols on the ground and the use of radios and other communication devices. Knowing how to communicate effectively and safely is essential for success and safety in bushcraft adventures, whether working in groups or dealing with emergency situations.

Chapter 10: Long Term Survival and Life Skills in the Wild

10.1 Introduction to long-term survival and life skills in the wild

Long-term survival in the wild requires a different set of skills and competencies than those required for short hikes or emergency situations. In this chapter we will look at planning and setting up a permanent base, farming and ranching techniques in the wilderness, long-term food storage, and developing a self-sustaining community in the woods.

10.2 Planning and organizing a permanent base

A permanent base is essential to ensure long-term survival in the wild. Here are some factors to consider when planning and organizing a base:

1. Location: Your base location should be close to essential resources such as water, food, and building materials. The base should also be located in an area protected from the weather and natural hazards.

2. Shelter: A solid, secure shelter is essential for protection from the elements and long-term comfort. The shelter should be constructed using available natural materials and environmentally appropriate construction techniques.

3. Field Layout: Field organization is important to ensure efficient and safe operation. This includes the design of areas dedicated to cooking, rest, work and storage.

4. Defense System: Having a defense system is essential to protect yourself from predators or intruders. This can include natural barriers such as hedges or fences as well as traps and alarms.

10.3 Agriculture and farming techniques in the wild

Agriculture and animal husbandry are essential skills to ensure a constant long-term supply of food in the wild. Here are some basic techniques:

1. Growing Plants: Growing edible plants such as fruits, vegetables, and grains can provide a sustainable food source. This includes soil preparation, planting, plant care and harvesting.

2. Animal Husbandry: Animal husbandry such as poultry, goats, and rabbits can provide you with meat, eggs, and milk. It is important to know the specific needs of animals and to ensure that they are given a suitable environment, food and proper care.

3. Sustainable hunting and fishing: Hunting and fishing can provide long-term sources of protein, but it's important to do so in a sustainable way. This means respecting local laws and hunting seasons, as well as practicing hunting and fishing techniques

4. Gathering and Propagation of Wild Plants: Gathering edible wild plants and learning how to propagate them can help diversify the diet and maintain food approval. It is important to know the local plants and learn to recognize edible and toxic ones.

10.4 Long-term food storage

Food storage is essential to ensure long-term food approval and to avoid waste. Here are some food preservation techniques:

1. Drying: Drying is a preservation method that involves removing water from food to prevent the growth of bacteria and mold. Foods such as fruit, vegetables, meat and fish can be dried in the sun, in the wind or in a dryer.

2. Smoking: Smoking is a preservation process that involves exposing food to smoke to kill bacteria and parasites and to add flavor. Meat and fish are the most commonly smoked foods.

3. Salting: Salting is a preservation method that involves adding salt to foods to dehydrate them and prevent the growth of bacteria. Meat and fish can be preserved with this method.

4. Fermentation: Fermentation is a preservation process which involves the transformation of foods thanks to the action of bacteria, yeasts or moulds. Some common fermented foods include sauerkraut, yogurt and cheese.

5. Vacuum bagging: Vacuum bagging is a preservation method that involves removing air from food packages to slow the growth of bacteria and prevent oxidation. This method is particularly effective for preserving meat and fish.

10.5 Development of a self-sufficient forest community

Creating a self-sustaining community in the woods can increase your chances of long-term survival and provide a more rewarding life experience. Here are some key elements to developing a community in the woods:

1. Cooperation and Teamwork: Cooperation and teamwork are essential to the success of a forest community. This includes the division of labour, the sharing of resources and mutual support.

2. Education and training: Education and training are essential to ensure that all community members have the skills and knowledge necessary to contribute to the survival of the group.

3. Resource Management: Effective resource management is critical to ensure community sustainability. This includes natural resource conservation, food resource planning, and waste management.

4. Safety and Security: The safety and security of the community is essential to ensure the survival and well-being of all members. This includes setting up barriers and defense systems, implementing safety protocols, and training all members in self-defense techniques.

5. Communication and Conflict Resolution: Effective communication and conflict resolution are key to maintaining a harmonious and cooperative atmosphere within the community. This includes creating open channels of communication, actively listening, and fostering a collaborative approach to problem solving.

6. Environmental Sustainability: Environmental sustainability is critical to ensuring the long-term survival of the community and the health of the surrounding ecosystem. This includes the protection of natural habitats, the promotion of sustainable agricultural practices and the responsible use of natural resources.

7. Developing a common culture and values: Creating a common culture and values can help strengthen the sense of identity and belonging within the community. This includes sharing traditions, rituals and practices that reflect the community's goals and ideals.

In conclusion, Chapter 10 of this bushcraft manual explored long-term survival and life skills in the wild, including planning and organizing a permanent base, wilderness farming and ranching techniques, conservation long-term food supply and the development of a self-sufficient forest community. Developing these skills and knowledge can greatly increase the chances of long-term success and well-being in nature, allowing individuals and communities to thrive and live in harmony with their surroundings.

CONCLUSIONS

This bushcraft handbook offers a comprehensive overview of the skills and knowledge needed to survive and thrive in the wild. From building shelters and starting fires, to obtaining food and managing water, each chapter provides detailed information and insights on how to live sustainably and responsibly in the wild. Orientation and navigation, first aid, tool making, communication and long-term survival are also essential aspects of a successful life in the wild. Learning and mastering these skills can enrich one's outdoor experience and provide a greater understanding of our relationship to our surroundings.

Crafty Ink **Manolo**